How to Read Music
(or how to make it in the Opera Big Time)

by Michael Adamczyk

Contents

Reading Music 101

Reading music is quite simple. People have been doing it for hundreds of years. There have been efforts to change the system but nobody has succeeded yet. Once you are shown what is going on reading music is very easy.

We will divide our task into two parts which will be melody and rhythm. We'll start with the rhythm part. The hardest part of this endeavor is remembering how to spell the word rytm. Otherwise it is really simple.

We know how division works in arithmetic so we follow the same procedure. If we have something that is whole we can divide it into halves. Then into quarters and sixteenths and so on. The same with music rhythm. On the next page you will see a whole note which takes up a whole measure. Wait! What's a measure? We divide a song into measures to show how the beats or sounds flow in a song. As you look at the next page you see two numbers: 4/4.

The numbers are in the first measure. There is also a fat note which takes up the entire measure. Notice we have five measures in the top first line which is called a staff. Below is another staff also with a 4/4 at the beginning. What do these numbers mean? I'm glad you asked. The top number (4) tells you that there are four beats in every measure and the bottom number (4) tells you that a quarter note gets one of those beats. Just like in math 4/4 would equal 1. As a matter of fact you can see in the second staff each measure has four numbers and only four. So 4/4 means we have 4 quarter notes in each measure. Really? Is music that boring? Well, you know the answer to that stupid question. A song or tune is made up of different rhythms or note lengths to make it interesting. You can see in the second staff that even though each measure has only 4 beats we can fit other types of notes in each measure.

We will end with a practical example: *Frere Jacques*. It starts on the third staff and consists of two staves. Again we are in 4/4. The first two measures are all quarter notes. We have a longer note (half note) on the word *John* in the third and fourth measures. When we get to *morning bells are ringing* we must stick in a lot of short notes in a measure so there are eight notes to do this. Here is a question: How many measures are in Frere Jacques?

Reading Music 101

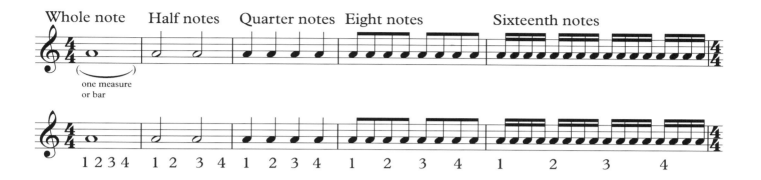

Frere Jacques

There are eight measures in this song. In each measure there are four beats or pulses; no more, no less. Notice the nice symmetry: each measure is repeated. Maybe this is why this is a fun song to sing.

The more you do to a note the shorter it gets. The whole notes is just sort of a circle. The half note adds a stem. The quarter note is filled in and the eight note has a flag added. The sixteenth note has two flags and so on.

Reading Music ¾ and Dots

You've found that at the beginning of a song there are always two numbers. One on top of the other. The top number tells you how many beats there are in a measure. The bottom number tells you what kind of note gets a beat. A measure divides the song into beat patterns. We had the example of "Frere Jacques" which had four beats in every measure and a typical measure had four quarter notes or an equivalent. It could be a whole note which is held for four counts or beats. It could be two half notes which have two beats each and so on.

There are songs which have different beat patterns. On page 5 you have a song which has only 3 beats in a measure. The song is "Down in the Valley". The top number is three and the bottom number is four. "Down in the Valley" has only three quarter notes in each measure. When you saw the "Frere Jacques" subdivision of notes starting with the whole note, (four beats) then dividing that into half notes, (each has two beats) then into quarter notes there was no three beat note. Here you meet an ingenious device. *The dot!* This little guy is really an addition sign. It follows a note and makes the note longer. In the song "Down in the Valley" there is a dot in the second measure that follows a half note. The note is now a three beat note. Any time we use a dot it makes the note longer by half of what the note is worth. Below is a chart showing how this works.

Whole note gets 4 beats ----------------------- with dot 6 beats.
Half note gets 2 beats --------------------------with dot 3 beats.
Quarter note gets 1 beat -------------------------with dot 1 1/2 beats.
Eight note gets ½ beat --------------------------with dot ¾ of a beat.
One sixteenth note gets ¼ beat ---------------------with dot 3/8 of a beat.

If this doesn't make sense to you, below the song "Down in the Valley" on page 4, there is a chart that may help.

Down in the Valley

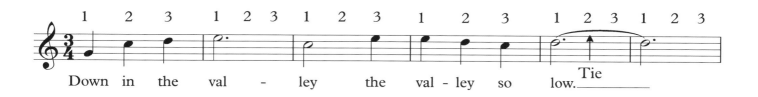

Down in the val - ley the val - ley so low. Tie

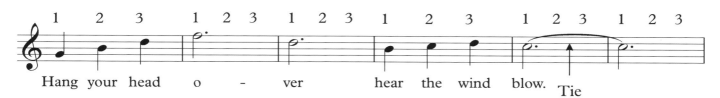

Hang your head o - ver hear the wind blow. Tie

You hold the note over
blow for 6 beats.

Dots are only good for a measure. If a note is held into the next measure you use a tie.

How dots work.

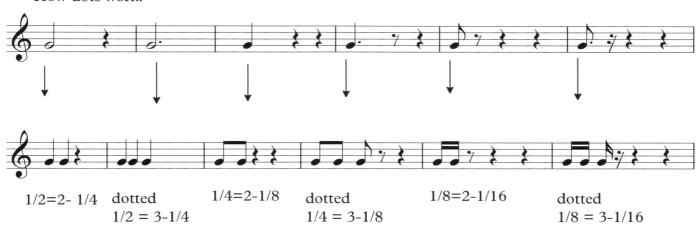

1/2=2- 1/4   dotted   1/4=2-1/8   dotted   1/8=2-1/16   dotted
1/2 = 3-1/4   1/4 = 3-1/8   1/8 = 3-1/16

Eight notes and sixteenth notes can be joined by a beam or have a flag.

2 eight notes   =   two eight notes.

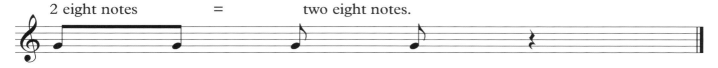

A New Time Signature

You've seen how the time signature works. The top number tells you how many beats in a measure and the bottom number tells you what kind of note gets the beat. Here is another time signature: 6/8. You will have six beats in every measure and the eight note gets one of the beats. On page 6 you have a familiar tune in 6/8. A quarter note with a dot is equal to 3 eight notes as seen in the chart on page 4. "Greensleeves" starts with one eight note, which is called a *pick up note.* Many songs start this way. You will also notice that the very last measure has only 5 beats. There is only 1 beat at the beginning of the song and there are 5 beats in the end measure which makes the 6 beats. Music likes to even itself out.

At first there seems to be difficult rhythms in this melody but on close inspection you can see there is a lot of repetition. In measure 1, 5, 9, and 13 the rhythm is the same on the fourth, fifth, and sixth beats. Over the word *love* in the first measure there is a dotted eight note which makes the note longer. It is followed by the short sixteenth note which comes just before the sixth beat over the word *you.* Again the same rhythm is used in measures 3, 7, 11, and 15.

The curved lines seen through the song are called slurs. They are there to show that one syllable is used for two or more notes. You can see this in measure 1 over the word *love* and in measure 2 over the word *wrong.* Slurs look like ties but they are always between different notes whereas ties are always between the exact same notes.

In a time signature you can have a 5, 7, 9, or 12 as the top number but these are not common. The bottom numbers are usually 4, 2, or 8. The most common time signatures are 4/4, 3/4, and 2/4. The 2/4 tells you that there are only 2 beats in each measure and the quarter note gets one of the beats. In some older music there are 4/2 and 3/2 time signatures. They are quite rare these days.

Greensleeves

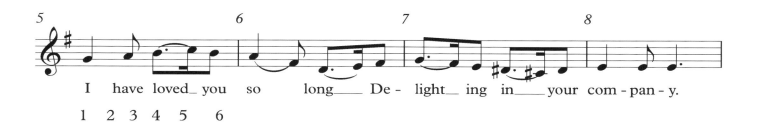

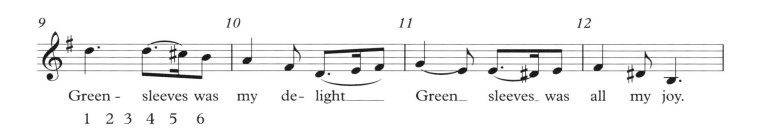

Rests

When you were discovering how dots work on page 4, you may have noticed some strange marks or signs. Those are rests or the absence of sound. Music notation is quite precise. If at the beginning of a song it says there will be four quarter notes in each measure (4/4) there won't be five or three, or six; only four beats. When there is an absence of sound it has to be accounted for. These no-sounds are called *rests.*

On page 9 we have a chart showing the types of notes and their equivalent rests. For example, in measure 1 there is a whole note. In measure 2 there is a whole rest. The whole note and the whole rest are counted for 4 beats because you are in 4/4 time.

In measures 19 and 20 on the bottom of page 9 are two examples of how this works. The time signature is 3/4 so you have three quarter notes per measure. You have two quarter notes in measure 19 but where is the third beat? That's where the quarter rest comes in. In reality we have two sounds and one silent beat. The same in measure 20, there is a sound that is held for two beats and a beat of silence. Remember there are three beats in each measure and they have to be accounted for.

Look! Look! Why is there an extra time signature in measures 10 and 18? (Wow! There are a lot of questions!) The time signatures change in the next measures (measures 11 and 19) and the time signatures in 10 and 18 are warnings about these changes. There are some songs that change their time signature in the middle of the song but tunes like that are not too common.

You are probably wondering when you look at the chart on page 9 why there are two half rests in measure 4. Why not put a whole rest? (you're pretty smart). In actuality that is how it is done. If nothing happens in a whole measure you would use a whole rest. Any time you have an empty measure you can use a whole rest.

Be careful with the 6/8 time signature. Remember the bottom number stands for the unit that gets one beat. This changes the counting in the measures. Six beats and each eighth note gets one beat.

Reading Music - Rests

Melody

You have learned about the numbers at the beginning of a song that show how the notes are made into the rhythmic structure of that song. Now you will find out about the melody part. Good news! It's even easier. The music notation is really a picture of the entire melody laid out in front of you. If the notes go up, the sound goes up and if the notes go down the sound goes down. It's that simple. There are a bunch of things that you should know to make this even easier. Let's start.

You've seen how music notation uses five lines and four spaces called a staff. On page 11 you see two staves hooked together and it is called the *Grand Staff,* which really means the big staff. The upper staff is called the treble or high staff and the lower is called the bass or low staff. The curlicue thing in the treble staff is called the "G" clef and the bass staff has a sign called the "F" clef.

More good news. Look at the lines and spaces. You name them with the same letters as our English alphabet. How easy! Between the bass and treble staves is the tone "C" and this particular tone is called <u>middle C</u> because it is right in-between the two staves. Middle C has its own little line called a leger line. You can see it just before the letter C in the middle of the two staves. Sometimes notes must go lower past middle C while staying in the treble clef. You can see this in the last staff on page 11. In the first measure there is a B which is the tone below middle C. In the second measure the A uses two leger lines. In the second measure of the bass staff you have tones that go lower than G so there is a leger line for the E. The last tones are going up past the bass staff: the D and E need leger lines, also.

Notice you use only seven letters of the alphabet. Can we get easier than that? Under the grand staff is a game for you to have fun with. Just look if the note is on a line or space then write the name of the line or space under the note. You even have an example.

The treble staff is used for high voices or squeaky instruments and the bass staff is used for low voices or growly instruments. Which do you use?

The Grand Staf

Treble or G clef

names of lines and spaces

Bass or F clef

Note Game

Scales

Now you should learn a little about scales. A scale is a musical ladder; you can go up and you can go down musically speaking. A scale is made of whole tones and half tones. Well, what does that mean? A whole tone is a whole step and a half tone is a half-step. Are we going crazy? What does that stuff mean? Well, let's take the song you already used on page 3. It's used again on page 13. If you sing or hum the first two tones of "Frere Jacque", the ones that go *Are You,* this is a whole step. Then when you go from *you sleep* that's another whole tone or whole step. This step business is similar to walking. When you walk you must move – you go from one spot to another. The same in music. You can't have a step if you stay on the same tone, just like standing in the same place, you have to move from one tone to another. A whole tone and a whole step are the same, in case you were wondering.

Below "Frere Jacque" there is a "C" scale. It's called that because it starts on C and ends on C. If you put numbers under the tones of the C scale you will notice that all the steps are whole steps except the ones between 3 – 4 and 7 – 8. This type of scale is called a *major* scale. It's not any better than any other scale that's just its name - *major.* As you also see below your numbered scale there's a *Do, Re, Mi.* You can use either one. When you sing or hum a scale you can hear the closeness of the two tones 3 and 4 (Mi and Fa). If you can't it is no big deal; it's kind of subtle. 7 and 8 (ti and do) are a bit easier to hear. Like anything that you are learning the more you study the subject the easier it gets. As the Germans say: "Übung macht den Meister."

When a person starts a scale on a different tone, adjustments must be made to keep the pattern correct. You can see how sharps are added to the D scale and a flat for the F scale.

Keyboard

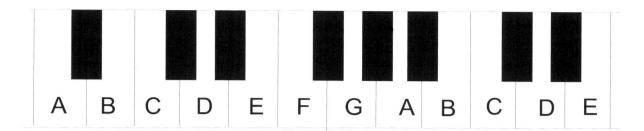

The A Minor Scale

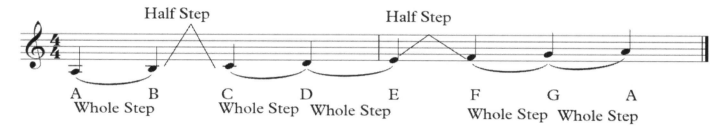

The C Major Scale

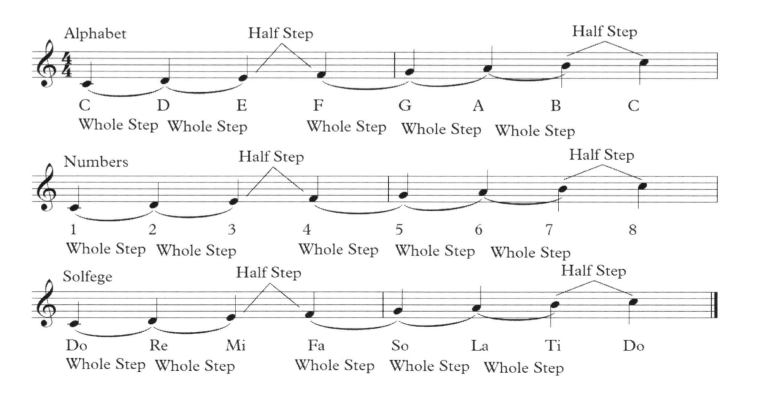

More on Scales

The C scale (C D E F G A B C) has a half step between the third and fourth, seventh and eight steps of the scale. The half steps are between E and F and B and C. Going down the scale C B A G F E D C, the half steps are still the same. If you use numbers, the half steps going down the scale would be between 8, 7 and 4, 3. You should remember this. How about: **B**e **C**areful of **E**very **F**act. That should work. B, C, E, F. Why the big deal? You'll find out now. Here are two more musical symbols that are very important. Sharp (#) and flat (b). A sharp raises a tone by a half step and a flat lowers a tone by a half step. If we have the two tones E and F (remember your saying; **B**e **C**areful of **E**very **F**act.) and you want to sing a whole step higher from E you can't do that because ordinarily the distance between E and F is a half-step. So here's what you do – you raise the F by using a sharp. Two half steps make a whole step. Now you have E to F sharp which is a whole step. In reality you are jumping over the F. Does this seem weird and convoluted? You bet. Here's why. Music notation like any language has evolved. Let's get back to sharps and flats.

On page 15 is a Christmas song which uses a scale type melody. It starts on C and works its way down the scale. Notice where the half steps are. You're right again! Between C and B (Joy to) and F and E (the Lord). You could say between the 8th, 7th and 4th and 3rd. This is probably why "Joy to the World" is easy to sing. You can sing it high or you can sing it low, whatever is comfortable for your voice. When you write it down it becomes problematical. (Whew! Big word!) Remember that music notation is very precise. If you start "Joy to the World" higher perhaps on G, the tone above the F on the treble staff, it starts to get weird. You can see in the second staff that is called "*Bad Song*" The melody should have a half step between the 8th and 7th steps. The half step is now between the F and E, the 7th and 6th steps (to the). Wow! What to do? There's still a half step between the C and B. In this case it's the 4th and 3rd steps. You're O.K. there. This is where you will use a sharp to fix everything. (Hoo Ray!) You put a sharp in front of the F and that sharp raises the F a half step. This makes a half step between the G and F sharp which is what you need to make the song correct. You now have the 8th and 7th half steps where they belong and this is shown in the version on the 3rd staff called "*Corrected Song*".

"Frere Jacques" starts with whole steps and this is shown in the lower staves. If you start the song on different tones you must make changes. Does this mean that every time you sing a song you have to put in sharps and flats? No. This is all done for you by composers and music arrangers. However you really want to know what's going on in music notation. In the next pages you will find out all sorts of other neat things to help.

Joy to the World!

Nice Song

Joy to the world, the Lord is come! Let earth re - ceive her King!

Bad Song

Joy to the world, the Lord is come! Let earth re - cieve her King!

Corrected Song

Joy to the world, the Lord is come! Let earth re - ceive her King!

Frere Jacques

Are you sleep -ing are you sleep -ing Bro - ther John? Bro - ther John?

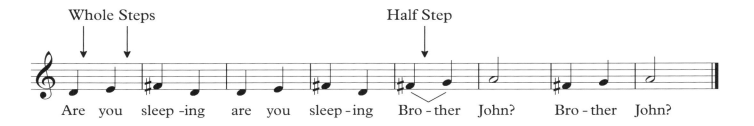

Are you sleep -ing are you sleep -ing Bro - ther John? Bro - ther John?

Key Signatures

Now you have another new term. *Key Signatures* When you use a certain scale to sing or play a song you say you are in that key. Here's a nice example. You sing "Joy to the world!" and you use the C scale. The C scale uses no sharps or flats; you're singing it in the key of C. The song could be moved higher or lower. Start higher on the scale of G. It's then in the key of G. Simple? Yes Sir! (or Yes Ma'am!) You learned that each line and space on the staff has an alphabetical name. You can use a scale on any one of the lines or spaces. That scale takes the name of the line or space. If you start a scale on the bottom line of the treble staff; that would be an E scale.

If you start a scale on the second space from the bottom on the treble staff, what would you call that scale? Wow! Right again. It would be an A scale. You can put a scale on any line or space.

On page 17 you see how "Frere Jacques" needs a sharp at the beginning (the third tone) to make whole steps so the song will sound right. In the top staff you needed a sharp every time you came to a C to make a whole step between the 2nd and 3rd steps of the scale. This has to be done for all the Cs. Musicians like to take short cuts so they put a C# at the beginning of the staff and you have to remember <u>all Cs are sharped</u>. This in turn becomes a *Key Signature*. If you are using the A scale. The sign for the A scale is three sharps. You can see this in the third staff called "Frere Jacques in A". The scale of A needs three sharps to sound right and this becomes the sign of A.

If you start "Frere Jacques" using a D scale you would use two sharps in the key signature as seen in the last staff of "Frere Jacques in D". This may seem confusing but there are only a few keys that people and musicians like to use. After a while it will become easier and easier.

Key Signatures

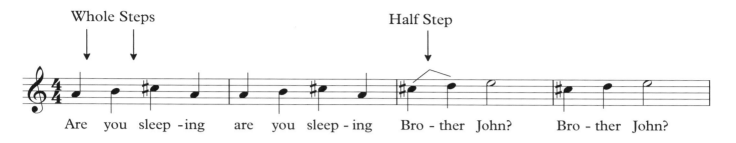

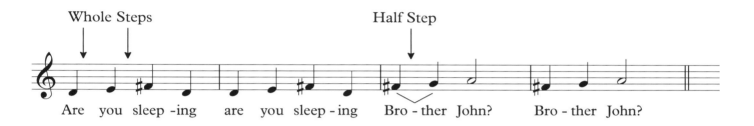

Frere Jacques in A

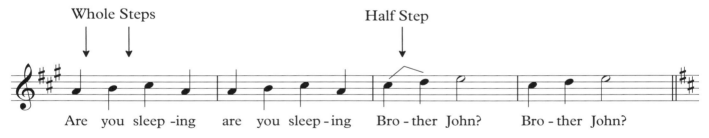

Frere Jacques in D

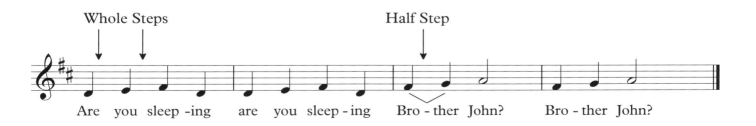

Chromatic Scale

On page 19 you have a Chromatic scale. It is a scale of all half steps. It really isn't used that often and is used for some special effects. The thing to notice is when the scale goes up you use sharps and when the scale goes down you use flats. There are instances when this rule is not always observed but you get the main idea. You can start a song on any one of those tones. For example you could use the C# (the second tone in the first measure) or the Gb (the second tone in the second staff first measure) The truth is that you will see songs in just a few keys such as C, F, G and Eb. These are scales that fit nicely in the voice range of humans.

How do you know what scale is being used? I'm glad you asked. On page 16 you learned about <u>Key Signatures.</u> At the beginning of a song you might see some sharps or flats. Those are <u>Key Signatures.</u> That's exactly what they are: signatures or signs of scales. When you put your signature on something you're saying that document or whatever belongs to you. So we have one sharp at the beginning of a song that tells you the song is in the key of G. Two sharps you are in the key of D and so on. Do you have to memorize all this stuff? Certainly not. You'll learn some tricks. Here's one right now. When you see sharps in the key signature take the last sharp to the right, go to the next higher tone and that's the key you're in. On page 19 you have some examples.

Why does the last measure have an A in the middle of the staff while all the previous ones have them high on the staff and what are those funny signs in the last staff ? Whoa! One question at a time. The A can be on a high line or space. That A is called the key tone or "Do". In this case all A's are called "Do" because you would be using the A scale. Those funny signs are called *naturals.* A natural takes away a sharp or a flat and puts the tone into its original position. The key of A has three sharps- the naturals took them all away.

Chromatic Scale

Key of E   Key of D   Key of G   Key of A

Last Sharp   Last Sharp   Last Sharp   Last Sharp

For flat keys take the last flat from the right and count down four. That tone is the key. The key of C has no sharps or flats in its key signature. When you are counting in music the first thing you talk about is number 1. For example in the key of F, if you start with the Bb on the middle line you would call number one then count down four until you got to F.

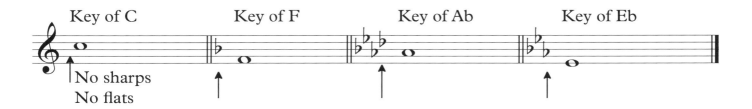

Key of C   Key of F   Key of Ab   Key of Eb

No sharps
No flats

Repeat Signs and Endings

You have on page 21 some important items. You have a song "Aupres de ma Blonde" that starts before measure 1. You would sing or play until the end of measure 4. The two dots at the right of measure 4 mean to repeat: go back to measure 1 and do it again. Even the eighth note that starts the song is in measure 4. After you repeat measures 1 to 3 you skip measure 4 and go directly to measure 5. That's what the 2 above the bracket means. You call that the second ending. You continue singing until you get to measure 13. Yep, you guessed it. There's a repeat sign that tells you to go back to measure 10. Again we have a 1st ending. After you repeat from measure 10 you skip measures 12 and 13. The 2nd ending, measures 14 and 15, end the song at the final double bar.

The song "All Through the Night" you repeat measures 16 through 19. When you get to measure 23 you go back to the beginning of the song (D.C.) and end where it says *Fine*.

In the song "Long, Long Ago" you sing all the way to where it says D.S. Then go back to the sign and repeat that part until the end *Fine*.

Below is a song which is in four part harmony. You see these in hymnals and song books. Soprano, the highest, with the note stems up. Alto, the lower part on the treble staff with the note stems down. In the bass staff the notes with the stems up are sung by the tenor. The lowest, with the stems down are sung by the bass.

Hark! The Harold Angels Sing.

Mendelsson

Aupres De Ma Blonde

All Through the Night

Long, Long Ago

Fine

Here you are at the end of these lessons but at the beginning of more musical adventures. What if you come across a melody and have no instrument to play it. Well you learned a lot and now it's time to use what you learned. On page 23 we have a song to use. First look at the time signature. Hmm. Two beats to the measure and a quarter note gets a beat. Hey! What's going on in the second staff? Oh, those are triplets and you squeeze three notes into the space of two. They always have a number 3 above or below to avoid confusion. Look at the key signature. Hmm. Two sharps. Take the last sharp to the right and go to the next line or space. The song is in D. Always, always, always look at the last tone. Yes, this song is in the key of D. Ninety-eight percent of songs like to end on the D<u>o</u> of the scale. If the tone or note does not match the key signature then the song is in the relative minor key. It would end on <u>La.</u> Your song on page 23 even starts on do. The rest of the song has the syllables for *sight singing* written out for you. You can use the do re mi or the numbers. This is very similar to reading a foreign language. At first it seems tedious and impossible but like any other endeavor it becomes easier with practice. As the Romans said "Perfectus usus facit." or as the Germans would say "Übung macht den Meister"

The song "Diebus Antiquis" is in 4/4 and in the key of F all right, but it does not start on do. What to do? Sing to yourself "do" then go down the scale (do ti la so). So is your starting tone. So-do. Continue: So-do, do do (re) mi. You think of do re mi but skip the re. You sing: So-do, do do-mi. Work your way through the song in this manner. It may take a few days but maybe not.

Ordinis Vestri Ordinis Trahentibus Navem

do do do re mi mi re mi fa so
1 1 1 2 3 3 2 3 4 5

triplets

do do do so so so mi mi mi do do do so fa mi re do.
8 8 8 5 5 5 3 3 3 1 1 1 5 4 3 2 1

Diebus Antiquis

So do do do mi re do re mi do do mi so la la so mi mi do
5 1 1 1 3 2 1 2 3 1 1 3 5 8 8 5 3 3 1

re do re mi do la la so do la so mi mi do re do re la so mi mi so
2 1 2 3 1 6 6 5 1 6 5 3 3 1 2 1 2 6 5 3 3 5

la do so mi mi do re do re mi re do la la so do
6 8 5 3 3 1 2 1 2 3 2 1 6 6 5 1

Test

Starting below and on page 25 are some songs with no titles. See if you can identify some of them. Remember to look at the key signature and check it with the last tone. Songs like to end on *Do* or *La* depending if it is a happy song in a major scale or a song using a sad minor scale. If the last tone does not match the key signature then you are in a minor key. Take your time. If you have no clue what the tune might be come back to it later.

A lot of songs start on *So* and jump up to *Do* but they always like to end on *Do*. Some like to start on *Mi* and jump to *La* and end on *La* if it uses a minor scale. The names of the melodies are on page 26.

Test

Test Continued

Test Answers

_____ Silent Night

_____ Twinkle Twinkle Little Star

_____ When Johnny Comes Marching Home

_____ Yankee Doodle

_____ Jingle Bells

_____ America

Printed in Great Britain
by Amazon

33712187R00018